Melanie Danet

Practise Your Comparatives

D'Arcy Adrian-Vallance

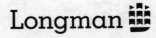

Longman

Contents

Introduction

Comparative adjectives

Superlative adjectives

Adverbs: Comparative and superlative

Comparative structures with adjectives, adverbs and quantifiers

Sayings and idioms

Answer key

Introduction

Comparative structures are a source of confusion to many students of English. *Practise Your Comparatives* provides clear examples and practice exercises for each aspect of these structures that is likely to cause problems for intermediate students.

Like the other workbooks in the *Practise Your* ... series, *Practise Your Comparatives* is suitable for self-access and classroom use and benefits from the following features:

- Language is practised in context to make it easier to see the meanings which determine the choice of a particular form.
- There is variety of exercise types, contexts and text types.
- The units are graded, from items with simple rules at the beginning of the book to more complex items towards the end.
- Pictures, artwork, diagrams, charts, realia and factual and sometimes amusing information all help to maintain interest as well as providing clear contexts and relating language to the real world.
- Personalisation exercises at the end of some units enable students to relate structures to their own lives and ideas. These more open-ended exercises are always preceded by controlled exercises in order to minimise the risk of errors. However, students may find it helpful to check their work in these exercises with a teacher.

It is hoped that this workbook will be found enjoyable and useful. The author and the publishers welcome comments from users.

1 Comparative adjectives: short words and long words

> **Short words and -y words**
> cheap – cheaper   happy – happier
> old   – older   noisy – noisier
>
> **Long words**
> expensive – more expensive
> modern   – more modern
>
> This shop is *cheaper than* that one.
> That shop is *more expensive than* this one.

1 A letter from New York

An English girl, Anna, went to New York on holiday. She wrote a letter to an English friend.

Choose one of these adjectives for each space in the letter on the next page. Write each one in its correct comparative form.

dangerous	tall	modern	straight	expensive	long	fast

Dear Mary,
    Here I am in New York! It's great! And it's very different to London: the roads are
¹ __longer__ and ² _____ than in London, the buildings are ³ _____ and ⁴ _____ and life here is ⁵ _____ – everyone is in a hurry! I thought the shops would be
⁶ _____ than in London but most things cost about the same. I was nervous too because people say that New York is
⁷ _____ than London, but I haven't had any trouble.
    See you soon!
                                    Love Anna

2 Anna liked New York so much that she decided to stay there. Now she is married to an American. Her friends from England sometimes ask her about her opinion of American people. Complete their questions with the words in brackets.

1 (nice) Do you think Americans _____ are nicer than _____ English people?

2 (ambitious) Do you think Americans _____ English people?

3 (kind) Do you think Americans _____ English people?

4 (interesting) Do you think Americans _____ English people?

5 (democratic) Do you think Americans _____ English people?

6 (happy) Do you think Americans _____ English people?

7 (religious) Do you think Americans _____ English people?

8 (generous) Do you think Americans _____ English people?

3 Think of some towns or cities that you know.
Write true sentences about them, using the words in brackets.

1 (small) _____

2 (interesting) _____

3 (cold) _____

4 (beautiful) _____

2 Spelling

1 hot – hotter big – bigger	**2** thick – thicker clean – cleaner
3 lucky – luckier healthy – healthier	**4** nice – nicer wide – wider

1 Final consonants (except *w* and *y*) are doubled if they follow a single vowel.
2 A final consonant is not doubled if it follows a consonant or two vowels.
3 A final *y* becomes an *i* if it follows a consonant.
4 If a word ends in *e*, only an *r* is added.

1 Write these adjectives and their comparative forms in the correct box below.

safe	cloudy	dry	bright	fit	keen	neat	wealthy
free	proud	late	thin	wet	sad	wide	sunny

hot – hotter

_____

_____

_____

_____

thick – thicker

_____

_____

_____

_____

lucky – luckier

_____

_____

_____

nice – nicer

safe - safer

_____

_____

_____

2 How many comparative adjectives can you find? Begin each word with a letter from column 1, then take a letter from column 2 and so on. Use each letter only once.

hotter _____   _____

_____   _____

_____   _____

_____   _____

_____   _____

	1	2	3	4	5	6	7
				I	R		
	B	O	A	T	T	R	
	H	I	T	E	R	R	
	S	G	F	G	E	R	
	U	L	G	Y	E	E	
	F	A	L	T	E	E	R

1	2	3	4	5	6
F	O	D	G	E	R
L	A	N	Y	E	R
W	U	S	E	R	
B	I	E	T	E	R
D	E	S	P	E	R
				I	R

3 British people frequently talk about the weather because the weather changes so often in Britain. Can you complete these typical conversations?

Yesterday   Today

1 A It isn't very nice today, is it?

  B No, *yesterday was nicer.*

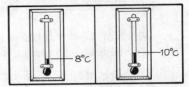

2 A It isn't very warm today, is it?

  B No, *but it's warmer than yesterday.*

3 A It isn't very sunny today, is it?

  B No, _____

4 A Isn't it fine today!

  B Yes, _____

5 A Oh dear! It's cloudy today.

  B Yes, _____

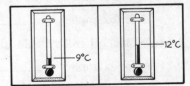

6 A It's cool today, isn't it?

  B Yes, _____

7 A It's been wet today, hasn't it?

  B Yes, _____

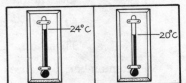

8 A It hasn't been very hot today, has it?

  B No, _____

3 Two-syllable adjectives: -er or more + adjective

1 Syllables

1-syllable words	2-syllable words	3-syllable words
blue clean	cru-el care-ful	beau-ti-ful dan-ger-ous

Which of the words below have two syllables? Write the number
of syllables in the brackets beside each adjective.

1 surprised (2)   6 ugly ( )   11 broad ( )
2 round (1)   7 sensible ( )   12 afraid ( )
3 serious ( )   8 strange ( )   13 different ( )
4 straight ( )   9 quiet ( )   14 excited ( )
5 useful ( )   10 thirsty ( )   15 horrible ( )

2 Adjective + -er or more + adjective?

Write one group of examples (a–e) in each of the spaces in the
grammar notes below.

(a) more surprised, more careful, more boring, more famous
(b) narrow, hollow, clever, bitter, simple, gentle
(c) happier, heavier, dirtier
(d) stupid, pleasant, common, handsome, polite
(e) quiet, cruel, tired

Grammar notes

Nearly all 2-syllable adjectives ending in -y form the comparative with -ier;

for example: 1_____

Most other 2-syllable adjectives form the comparative with more + adjective;

for example: 2_____

However, a few 2-syllable words can use either form.

They are (a) words which sound almost like 1-syllable words;

for example: 3_____

(b) words ending in -ow, -er and -le

for example: 4_____

(c) 5 other common words

These are 5_____

Remember: if you are not sure, use more + adjective. It is hardly ever wrong.

---

3 Right or wrong?

Here is a page from a student's exercise book. There are mistakes
in *six* of the sentences. Put a line through the mistakes and write
the corrections on the right. Do not put a line through a word
unless it is definitely wrong.

Comparatives

1 I'm cleverer than my brother.

2 New York's moderner than London.   *more modern*

3 Mary's pleasanter than Janet.

4 But Janet's more polite than Mary.

5 They're busier than we are.

6 Please be quieter!

7 You must be more gentle!

8 My sentence is correcter than yours.

9 This exercise is more easy than that one.

10 A lemon is more bitter than an orange.

11 You must be carefuler!

12 Why can't you be more honest?

13 Can you be exacter?

14 Don't make him more annoyed.

15 I was more surprised than he was.

16 This machine is simpler than the others.

17 This road's narrower than the others.

18 This is more urgent than that.

19 He gets stupider every day.

20 Can you come more early next time?

21 I'm handsomer than my brother.

22 Spain is drier than Britain.

4 One- two- and three-syllable adjectives

Examples

This is *older* than that.
It's *narrower* than that.
It's *more common* than that.
It's *more interesting* than that.

1 It is Mark's birthday tomorrow. Lisa has just bought a present for him. Use the words in brackets to complete Lisa's sentences.

MARK: What is it? Tell me!

LISA: If I tell you it won't be a surprise tomorrow.

MARK: I know but . . . Is it a record?

LISA: No. It's (expensive) ¹ _more expensive than that._

MARK: Really? It isn't a computer, is it?

LISA: You must be joking! It's (cheap) ² _____

MARK: Oh. A picture?

LISA: No. It's (useful) ³ _____

MARK: Useful? Oh, then it must be a jacket.

LISA: No. It's (small) ⁴ _____

MARK: A shirt!

LISA: No! It's (special) ⁵ _____

MARK: Oh, I can't guess.

LISA: Good!

MARK: Wait! I know! It's a book – one of those big Art books.

LISA: No. It's (necessary) ⁶ _____

MARK: Ah. A pair of trousers?

LISA: No. It's (informative) ⁷ _____

MARK: Informative? You mean it gives information. A video cassette?

LISA: No. It's (mechanical) ⁸ _____

MARK: Oh, I give up!

Can you guess what Lisa has bought?

2 Choosing presents

Read the information about eight people and then complete the
dialogue.

> Tim likes funny books.
> Andrea likes serious books, films and music.
> Lisa likes delicate jewellery and dark colours.
> Rick likes sweet things.
> Simon likes old things.
> Peter likes modern things.
> Paul likes useful things (especially for the kitchen).
> Angela likes bright colours and romantic films.

A Would Andrea like a funny book?

B She'd like 1 _something more serious than that._

A What about a box of chocolates for Rick?

B He'd like 2 _that._

A What would Andrea think of *A History of Western Philosophy?*

B She'd like 3 _____

A Do you think Tim would like a book about animals?

B He'd like 4 _____

A Would Tim like a book called *The World's Best Jokes?*

B He'd like 5 _____

A Now Angela: would she like a black hat?

B She'd like 6 _____

A OK. Now Lisa. She likes jewellery. What about a big black bracelet?

B She'd like 7 _____

A I've thought of the perfect present for Simon: an old sword!

B He'd like 8 _____

A Would Peter like an old sword?

B He'd like 9 _____

A What about a record for Paul?

B He'd like 10 _____

A What about a James Bond video cassette for Angela?

B She'd like 11 _____

A Would Lisa like a very small white bracelet?

B She'd like 12 _____

5 *More* or *less?*

> **Examples**
>
> Football is *more dangerous* than tennis.
> Tennis is *less dangerous* than football.

1 Who is speaking?

The pictures show what Peter, John, Jenny, Hazel and Sam did yesterday.
After each of the sentences (1–5), write the name of the person who is speaking.

Jenny went hang-gliding.

Peter went to the dentist.

John listened to a lecture.

Sam wrote a report.

Hazel went to a party.

1 'It was more frightening than the dentist but less uncomfortable.' _____ says.

2 'It was more painful than working and less profitable.' _____ says.

3 'It was less enjoyable than a holiday but more urgent.' _____ says.

4 'It was less noisy than a disco and it was easier to talk to people there.' _____ says.

5 'It was less exciting than a football match but more useful for my studies.' _____ says.

2 Write true sentences about the places and activities below.
Be careful! Some sentences are negative (*less*) and some are
positive (*more* or *-er*).

1 Golf | dangerous | football

   <u>Golf is less dangerous than football.</u>

2 Tennis courts | small | football pitches

   _____

3 Walking | tiring | running

   _____

4 Playing tennis | expensive | flying a plane

   _____

5 Discos | noisy | cinemas

   _____

6 Libraries | quiet | bookshops

   _____

7 Wrestling | violent | boxing

   _____

8 Polo | popular | football

   _____

9 Motor-cycle racing | peaceful | fishing

   _____

10 Motor-cycle racing | expensive | jogging

   _____

11 A swimming pool | warm | the sea

   _____

12 The sea | crowded | a public swimming pool

   _____

3 **What's your opinion?**

Write some more sentences (with *more* or *less*) about activities
and places.

1 _____ interesting _____

2 _____ exciting _____

3 _____ difficult _____

6 Negatives: *not as ... as*

> **Examples**
>
> A motorcycle is *not as* expensive *as* a car.
> A car is *not as* cheap *as* a motorcycle.
>
> (*less ... than* may be used with long adjectives but is
> not normally used with short adjectives.)

1 Look at the pictures of three film stars and then complete the
dialogues below, using the *not as* adjective *as* structure.

1 A Chris Carter's richer than Bernard Bjorg.

   B Yes, but *he isn't as rich as Alfie Anderson.*

2 A Bernard Bjorg's more attractive than Chris Carter.

   B Yes, but _____

3 A Alfie Anderson is more intelligent than Chris Carter.

   B Yes, but _____

4 A Alfie Anderson is younger than Bernard Bjorg.

   B Yes, but _____

5 A Alfie Anderson is stronger than Bernard Bjorg.

   B Yes, but _____

6 A Alfie Anderson's face is more sensitive than Chris Carter's.

   B Yes, but _____

2 Now write some sentences about some real film stars.

1 _____

2 _____

3 _____

3 Why is it cheaper?

In this exercise write an *as... as* sentence and, if possible, a *less ... than* sentence.

1

   (a) The cheaper chair _isn't as comfortable as the other one._

   (b) The cheaper chair _____

2

   (a) The cheaper car _is less comfortable than the other one._

3

   (a) The cheaper computer _____

   (b) The cheaper computer _____

4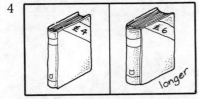

   (a) The cheaper book _____

5

   (a) The cheaper picture _____

   (b) The cheaper picture _____

6

   (a) The cheaper drill _____

   (b) The cheaper drill _____

7

   (a) The cheaper apples _____

7 Irregular adjectives and quantifiers

Adjectives	Quantifiers
bad – worse	much – more
good – better	many – more
far – further	little (quantity) – less
	few – fewer

1 Use one word from the box above to fill each space in the weather forecast below.

Good evening. Well, we've had very little sunshine today and we'll have even 1_____ sunshine tomorrow. There will be

2_____ cloud than there has been today and the wind will be stronger, especially in the north of England, where there will be storms and heavy rain.

   The south of England is 3_____ from the low pressure over Scotland, so the weather in the south will not be as

4_____ as in the north and there will be 5_____ storms in the south. However, it will remain 6_____ than usual for this time of year in all parts of the country.

   The good news is that there is high pressure coming across the Atlantic. This will bring some 7_____ weather by the weekend.

2 **What's the weather like where you are?**

Is it better than last month or not as good?
Is it cloudier? sunnier? hotter? cooler than last month?
Write some true sentences.

1 _____

2 _____

3 _____

3 Quantifiers

> **Examples**
>
> She buys *less* chocolate than I do.
> I buy *more*.
> She doesn't buy as *much* as I do.

Study the diagram below and then fill each space with *one or more* words.

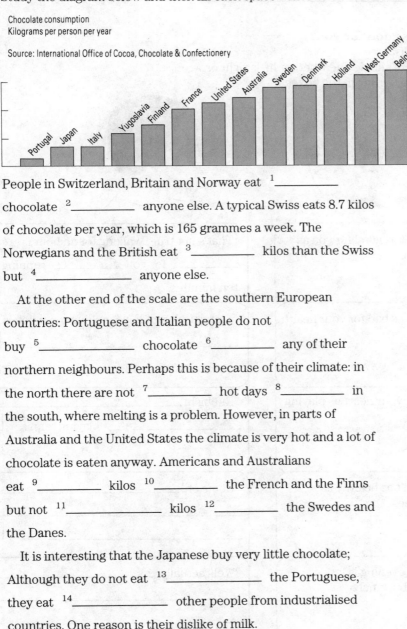

Chocolate consumption
Kilograms per person per year

Source: International Office of Cocoa, Chocolate & Confectionery

People in Switzerland, Britain and Norway eat ¹_____

chocolate ²_____ anyone else. A typical Swiss eats 8.7 kilos

of chocolate per year, which is 165 grammes a week. The

Norwegians and the British eat ³_____ kilos than the Swiss

but ⁴_____ anyone else.

   At the other end of the scale are the southern European

countries: Portuguese and Italian people do not

buy ⁵_____ chocolate ⁶_____ any of their

northern neighbours. Perhaps this is because of their climate: in

the north there are not ⁷_____ hot days ⁸_____ in

the south, where melting is a problem. However, in parts of

Australia and the United States the climate is very hot and a lot of

chocolate is eaten anyway. Americans and Australians

eat ⁹_____ kilos ¹⁰_____ the French and the Finns

but not ¹¹_____ kilos ¹²_____ the Swedes and

the Danes.

   It is interesting that the Japanese buy very little chocolate;

Although they do not eat ¹³_____ the Portuguese,

they eat ¹⁴_____ other people from industrialised

countries. One reason is their dislike of milk.

8 Negative and positive comparisons (regular and irregular)

Examples
Living in the country is *healthier* than living in the town. Living in the town isn't *as healthy as* living in the country.

1 Do you know what is good for you?

John and Peter always disagree.
Complete Peter's answers and decide whether he is right or wrong.
Write **R** for right or **W** for wrong in the boxes.

Walking for an hour isn't as good for you as running for ten minutes.

[1]That's not true. Walking for an hour is _____ for you _____ running for ten minutes. ☐

Smoking too much isn't as bad for your health as sleeping too much.

[2]You must be joking! Smoking too much is _____ ☐

Cycling isn't as good for your heart as playing tennis.

[3]Rubbish! _____ _____ playing tennis. ☐

Taking long holidays isn't as healthy as working hard all the time.

[4]Come on! _____ _____ _____ ☐

Eating a big meal in the evening is less fattening than having a big lunch.

[5]Well, actually, _____ _____ ☐

2 How calm and relaxed are you?

You can find out by answering the questions in this personality
quiz from a popular magazine.

Are you relaxed? Tick (√) the boxes and find out.	Yes. I agree	No. I don't agree
1 Doing something useful is more enjoyable than watching television.		
2 Playing for fun is less satisfying than playing to win.		
3 Being admired is nicer than being liked.		
4 Competing is more enjoyable than cooperating.		
5 Driving safely is less important than arriving on time.		
6 People who drive too slowly are worse than people who drive too fast.		
7 Chatting is less interesting than discussing work.		
8 Visiting important monuments is better than lying on the beach.		

Now look in the key section at the back of the book to find out about yourself.

3 Rewrite the sentences from Exercise 2, using *not as... as*.
Write YOUR opinion.

1 EITHER _Yes. Watching TV isn't as enjoyable as doing something useful._
  OR _No. Doing something useful isn't as enjoyable as watching TV._

2 _____ as _____

3 _____

4 _____

5 _____

6 _____

7 _____

8 _____

9 Adjective or quantifier + noun

Positive	Negative
a better job	not such a good job
better friends	not such good friends
more friends	not as/so many friends

1 Positive sentences

You are shopping. The shop assistant shows you some things that you do not like.

1   brim: too narrow

ASSISTANT: Would you like to try this hat?

YOU: Have you got one _with a wider brim ?_

2   collar: too high

ASSISTANT: Would you like to try this shirt?

YOU: Have you got one _____ ?

3   buckle: too large

ASSISTANT: What about this nice belt?

YOU: Have you got one _____ ?

4   legs: too short

ASSISTANT: These trousers are very good.

YOU: Have you got some _____ ?

5   handle: too small

ASSISTANT: Do you like this umbrella?

YOU: Have you got one _____ ?

6   buttons: too many

ASSISTANT: Would you like to try this coat?

YOU: Have you got one _____ ?

7   frames: too thick

ASSISTANT: These sunglasses are very popular.

YOU: Have you got some _____ ?

8   lapels: too wide

ASSISTANT: This is an extremely nice jacket.

YOU: Have you got one _____ ?

2 Now the assistant shows you some things you like.
Say why you prefer them to the things you saw before (in Exercise 1).

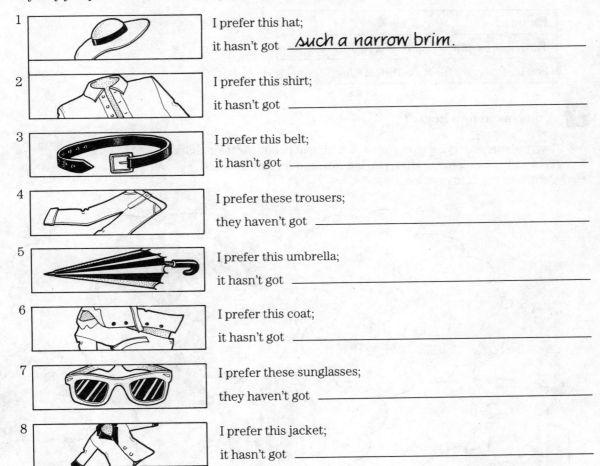

1 I prefer this hat;

it hasn't got ___such a narrow brim.___

2 I prefer this shirt;

it hasn't got _____

3 I prefer this belt;

it hasn't got _____

4 I prefer these trousers;

they haven't got _____

5 I prefer this umbrella;

it hasn't got _____

6 I prefer this coat;

it hasn't got _____

7 I prefer these sunglasses;

they haven't got _____

8 I prefer this jacket;

it hasn't got _____

3 Compare these two cars. Write about their engines, seats, boots and doors.

An old saloon car

big boot

4 doors

A new sports car

Very comfortable seats

A powerful engine

2 doors

1 The saloon car _____

2 The saloon car _____

3 The saloon car _____

4 The saloon car _____

10 Comparative adjective phrases

Examples
Tim's *more interesting* to talk to *than* Wayne.
Lee isn't *as easy* to work with *as* Clint.

1 A dog, a cat or a horse?

Two parents are trying to decide which animal to buy for their children.
They talk about looking after, playing with and feeding animals.
Complete the conversation.

WOMAN: Let's buy a dog for the children.

MAN: A cat would be (easy) ¹_____*easier to*_____ look _____*after than*_____ a dog.

WOMAN: But cats aren't (exciting) ²_____ play _____ dogs.

MAN: No, but cats are (cheap) ³_____ feed _____ dogs.

WOMAN: What the children would really like is a horse.

MAN: But horses are (expensive) ⁴_____ feed _____ cats and

dogs, and they're (difficult) ⁵_____ look _____ .

WOMAN: Oh! You disagree with me about everything! I sometimes wonder why you married me.

MAN: Because you're (nice) ⁶_____ be with _____ anyone

else!

2 Write an advertisement.

Use the information about each item to describe its advantages in one sentence.

1

Using this computer is simple.
You can also carry it easily.

It's *simpler to use and easier to carry than other computers.*

2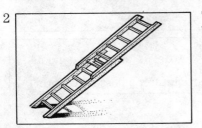

This ladder is safe when you stand on it.
You can store it conveniently, too.

It's _____

_____

3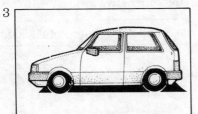

You can run this car cheaply.
You can also park it easily.

It's _____

_____

4

Sitting in this chair is comfortable.
And it's nice to look at.

It's _____

_____

5

Listening to this personal stereo is enjoyable.
Carrying it is easy.

It's _____

_____

6

Visiting this holiday resort is exciting.
Leaving it is difficult.

It's _____

_____

23

11 Superlative adjectives – short words and long words

Adjectives of 1-syllable and -y adjectives	2- or 3-syllable adjectives
old → (the) oldest early → (the) earliest	beautiful → (the) most beautiful useful → (the) most useful

A few 2-syllable adjectives
form the superlative with -*est*
and the comparative with -*er* (see Unit 3, Exercise 2)

Examples: Harrods is *the most famous* shop in London. ⎫ (Article + adjective + noun)
Harrods is not *the cheapest* shop in London. ⎭
Harrods is London's *most famous* shop. (No article after a possessive form)

1 Complete each sentence with one of the following adjectives in the superlative form.

dangerous   heavy   deep   tall   long   expensive   old   fast   intelligent   successful   loud   large

1 George MacAree, on the left of the picture is _____
man in Britain.

2 The man on the right, Christopher Greener, is Britain's
_____ man.

3 _____
_____
_____ spider
is the black widow, whose
bite can kill a man in a few
minutes.

4 The insect with _____ number of legs is a kind of
millipede which has 710 legs.

5 The world's _____ perfume costs £550 per
bottle.

6 _____ bridge in the world is in Izmir, Turkey. It
is more than 2,800 years old.

7 _____ part of the Pacific Ocean is 11 kilometres
below the surface.

8 Richard Latter, who died in 1914, had _____

beard in the world.

9 _____ of all songwriters have

been John Lennon and Paul McCartney.

10 _____ land animal is the cheetah, which can run

at nearly 100 kilometres per hour.

11 _____ insect, the cicada, can be heard at a

distance of 400 metres.

12 _____ sub-human animal on land

is the chimpanzee.

12 Spelling

The spelling rules for superlatives are similar to the rules for comparatives, except that the ending is *-est* instead of *-er*. (see Unit 2)

1 Crossword

Where the base form is given, write the superlative form.
Where the superlative form is given, write the base form.

ACROSS
  2 close
  4 busy
  6 bluest
  7 hungry
  8 wisest
  9 thirsty
 13 soft
 14 tame
 15 tightest
 16 slow
 22 low
 23 wet

DOWN
  1 big
  3 sour
  5 sticky
  7 hot
  8 white
 10 safe
 11 simple
 12 fit
 17 widest
 18 softest
 19 fewest
 20 hottest
 21 wettest

13 Irregular adjectives and quantifiers

Adjectives	Quantifiers
bad – (the) worst good – (the) best far – (the) furthest	much – (the) most many – (the) most little – (the) least

Examples: She's *the best,* friend he's got.
She's his *best* friend. (No article after the possessive form)

Read the information below.
Then complete the sentences with a superlative *and an article if possible.*

1 Mieko, Petra and Marie have just flown into London Airport from
different parts of the world. Petra is now further from home than
Marie but not as far from home as Mieko is. Surprisingly, the
person who is further from home than the others hasn't the most
luggage. But that person has more luggage than Petra. Petra had
quite a good trip. Marie says it was the worst flight she has ever
had. However, Mieko had a worse flight than Marie did: her plane
was delayed for 14 hours.

1 Mieko has travelled _____ distance.

2 This has been Marie's _____ flight.   4 Marie has _____ luggage.

3 Mieko has had _____ flight of all.   5 Petra has _____ luggage.

2 Mieko, Petra and Marie are all going to study English at a language
school in Oxford. One of these students is going to live in a school
house. In fact she has got the best room in the house. It is quite
large and has a nice view. The other two students will live with
English families as paying guests, which will be cheaper. One of
the families is not far from the school; the other family is on the
other side of the city but there is a good bus service. The cheapest
room is the furthest one from the school and it is quite large.
Marie will have to spend more money on bus fares than Petra but
less money on her accommodation. Petra's room is not the most
expensive one but it is larger than Mieko's.

1 Marie is going to spend _____ money on her accommodation.

2 Petra's room has _____ space.

3 Mieko will be in the school's _____ room.

4 Marie's room is _____ one from the school.

5 Marie will have to spend _____ money on bus fares.

27

14 Superlative adjectives: mixed types

1 Advantages and disadvantages

Three students are going to share a flat. The flat has three rooms,
a big kitchen and a bathroom. You must help them to decide
which room each student should have.
First look at the plan of the flat.

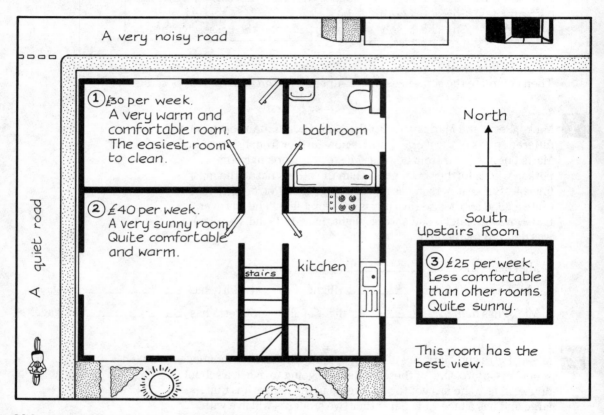

A very noisy road

A quiet road

① £30 per week.
A very warm and
comfortable room.
The easiest room
to clean.

② £40 per week.
A very sunny room
Quite comfortable
and warm.

stairs

kitchen

bathroom

North

South
Upstairs Room

③ £25 per week.
Less comfortable
than other rooms.
Quite sunny.

This room has the
best view.

Make notes of the advantages and disadvantages of each room.
Use the *superlative* form of the following adjectives and phrases:

warm   noisy   quiet   sunny   little sunlight   cheap   expensive large   a good view   small   comfortable   easy to clean many windows   good for working in   near the kitchen

Room 1	**Room 2**	**Room 3**
warmest		

2 Read about the three students. Then fill each space with one of the words or phrases from your notes in Exercise 1. Use an article (*the*) where possible.

PETE is the most serious student. He spends a lot of time working in his room so he likes to have a good view from his window. He has not got much money.

JOHN is the friendliest of the three students. He likes to invite a lot of friends to his room. He enjoys cooking, hates dark rooms and has plenty of money.

EDDY is rather lazy. He likes to do as little as possible. He likes warm rooms.

For PETE, the poor student, ¹_____ room would be the most suitable. I think he would like this room because he studies hard and this room is ²_____ . It is the furthest one from the road so it is ³_____ room. He would also like it because it has ⁴_____ . The only disadvantage is that it is ⁵_____ room.

I think ⁶_____ room would be the best room for JOHN because he is the one with the most friends and so he needs a large room in which to entertain them. The room is also ⁷_____ one to the kitchen and John likes cooking. Sunshine is one of the most important things for John and this is the flat's ⁸_____ room because it has ⁹_____ windows and faces south. It is also ¹⁰_____ room but John can afford it.

EDDY, the lazy one, would prefer not to have to walk upstairs to his room. He hates cold rooms so he would like to have ¹¹_____ room. He also hates cleaning and this room is ¹²_____ Comfort is important for Eddy, and this is ¹³_____ room. Eddy does not study much so he would not mind that it is the flat's ¹⁴_____ room. He stays in bed for much of the day and would not mind that the room gets ¹⁵_____

15 Superlative or comparative?

Examples	
He is *the best*	*in* the team.
	of the eleven players.
He is *better than* He is not *as good as*	the ten others.

The British Royal Family

The Queen and Prince Philip

Edward born 1964

Anne born 1950

Andrew born 1960

Charles born 1948

1 Complete the sentences, using one of the phrases from the box in each sentence.

1 Charles is older than _____

2 Anne is not as old _____

3 Anne is not the oldest in _____

4 Anne is the second oldest of _____

5 Andrew is the second oldest of _____

6 Andrew is not as young _____

7 Edward is younger _____

8 Edward is the youngest _____

the four.
the family.
the brothers.
his brothers.
than all the others.
of all.
as Charles.
as Edward.

2 Have *you* got brothers or sisters?

Write some *-er* and *-est* sentences about your family or about another family.

1 _____

2 _____

3 _____

4 _____

3 **The Planets**

Look at the diagram carefully and then complete the text. Use a comparative structure (positive or negative) or a superlative structure (+ preposition if necessary).

On the edge of our family of planets, or solar system, is Pluto, which is (cold) [1] *the coldest of* all the planets and (far) [2] _____ the sun.

Surprisingly, (hot) [3] _____ planet is not Mercury although no other planet is (close) [4] _____ the sun. Mercury, with a surface temperature of about 420°C is (hot) [5] _____ Venus, which has a surface temperature of about 475°C.

Mercury is (small) [6] _____ the nine planets and Jupiter is (large) [7] _____ the solar system.

Mercury, Mars and Venus are similar to Earth in some ways. Venus is (close) [8] _____ to Earth. However it is less similar to Earth than Mars is. Although Venus is a small planet, it looks (bright) [9] _____ the four large planets. In fact, of all the planets it is (bright) [10] _____ in our sky.

Look at the diagram again and check that it agrees with your sentences.

31

16 Superlatives and comparatives with *ever* and *never*

Superlative		
This is the	*worst* *most horrible* *best*	meal I've ever eaten.
Comparative		
I've never eaten *such a*	bad horrible good	meal (*as* this).

1 What are the people in the pictures saying or thinking?
Write sentences using the words in brackets.

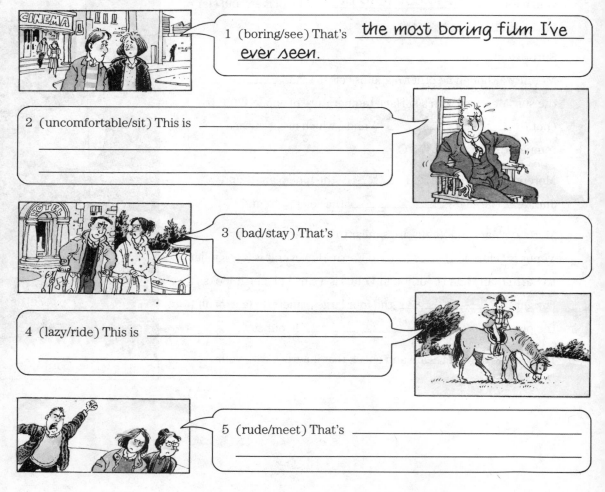

1 (boring/see) That's the most boring film I've ever seen.

2 (uncomfortable/sit) This is _____

3 (bad/stay) That's _____

4 (lazy/ride) This is _____

5 (rude/meet) That's _____

2 Write each sentence from Exercise 1 in a different way, beginning with *I've never*...

1 I've _never seen such a boring film._____

2 I've _____

3 I've _____

4 I've _____

5 I've _____

3 What might you say in the following situations?
Write two things that you could say.

1 You have just seen a very good film at the cinema.

  (a) That's _the best film I've ever seen._____

  (b) I've _never seen such a good film._____

2 You see a beautiful view.

  (a) It's _____

  (b) I've _____

3 You have met a very generous person.

  (a) He's _____

  (b) I've _____

4 You've just talked to a very interesting person.

  (a) She's _____

  (b) I've _____

5 You have just been to a very nice party.

  (a) That's _____

  (b) I've _____

4 Write true sentences about yourself.

1 _____ is the best film I've ever seen.

2 _____ is the worst _____ .

3 _____ book _____ .

4 _____ place _____ visited.

5 _____ .

17 One of the -*est*

> The Amazon is *one of the longest* rivers in the world.
>
> The Amazon is *the second longest* river in the world.

1   Read these fascinating facts and then underline the correct words in the exercise.

The richest people in Britain and the USA	The most common words in English	The most populated cities in the world	The longest rivers in the world
1 Gordon Getty (USA) 2 Queen Elizabeth 3 The Duke of Westminster 4 Sam Walton (USA)	1 the 2 of 3 and 4 to	1 Mexico 2 Shanghai 3 Tokyo 4 Cairo	1 The Nile 2 The Amazon 3 The Yangtse 4 The Zaire

One of ^{1} { a / the } richest ^{2} { people / person } in the world ^{3} { is / are } the Duke of Westminster, who owns part of London. He is still in his late thirties and is the ^{4} { two / second } richest ^{5} { people / person } in Britain.

Prepositions are ^{6} { some / one } of the most common ^{7} { word / words } in English. 'Of' is ^{8} { second / the second } most frequently used word ^{9} { of / in } the language and 'to' is also ^{10} { one / four } of the most frequently occurring words.

One of the largest ^{11} { city / cities } in the world ^{12} { is / are } Cairo in Egypt. However, Shanghai and Tokyo are larger. They are the second and third ^{13} { of the largest / largest } cities ^{14} { of / in } the world. Mexico City is ^{15} { the largest / the first largest } .

2 **What do you know about ...**

1 The Yangtse? *It's one of the longest rivers in the world.*

2 The word 'and'? *It's one*

3 Sam Walton? _____

_____

4 Shanghai? _____

_____

Sam Walton

3 Complete the conversations.

1 Is the Duke of Westminster the richest person in Britain?

No, *he's the second richest person.*

2 Is the Zaire the longest river in the world?

No, _____

3 Is Tokyo the most populated city in the world?

No, _____

4 Is 'of' the most common word in English?

No, _____

4 Write some sentences about people and places that you know.

1 _____ is _____ interesting cities in my country.

2 _____ is _____ people that I know.

3 _____ the second oldest person in my family/my class.

4 _____

18 Zero article superlatives

This drink is *best* in cold weather. (It's not so good in hot weather.)
This drink is *the best* I've ever tasted. (It's better than other drinks.)

This hotel is *least expensive* in winter. (It's cheaper than it is in summer).
This hotel is *the least expensive* in the town. (It's cheaper than other hotels.)

Most (without *the*) sometimes has the meaning of nearly all, the majority.
Examples: Most cars have four wheels.
            Most of my friends have cars.

1 Write *the* in the spaces where possible. (Sometimes you must leave the space empty.)

Every year millions of people visit Britain as tourists, and ¹_____ most

visitors spend some time in the capital, London, which has some of ²_____

most interesting sights in the world. You can see ³_____ most of them at

any time of the day. The Tower of London is the monument which has

⁴_____ most visitors.

   ⁵_____ best time to visit Britain is probably in late Spring, Summer or

early Autumn. The weather is ⁶_____ best in July and August (although

even then it is certainly not ⁷_____ best weather in Europe!) However,

the museums and monuments are ⁸_____ most crowded in August, and

London can be unpleasantly hot at this time. So this may be ⁹_____ best

time to get out of the city and see the rest of the country.

2 Write sentences using the words given.

1 Geneva / one of / modern cities in Europe.

Geneva is one of the most modern cities in Europe.

2 Venice / romantic city / Europe.

_____

3 Paris / beautiful / Spring.

_____

4 September / best time / visit India.

_____

5 Australia / hottest when it is Winter in Europe.

_____

6 Spain / popular destination for British tourists.

_____

7 Americans, Germans and French people / frequent visitors to Britain.

_____

8 Public transport in London / expensive / Europe.

_____

9 The beaches of Europe / crowded / August.

_____

10 There / something interesting to see / most countries.

_____

19 Comparative and superlative adverbs (regular)

carefully – more carefully – most carefully
easily – more easily – most easily
slowly – more slowly – most slowly
Terry drives *more dangerously than* Jane but not *as*
dangerously as Erica.
Erica drives *(the) most dangerously* of all. (the = formal; ~~the~~ = less formal)
People drive *most dangerously* when they are tired.

Short adverbs (*loudly, slowly*, etc) are often given *-er* and *-est* endings in spoken
English: 'He shouted *loudest* of all.' instead of *'most loudly'* or
'*the most loudly*'.
'He drives *slower* than me.' instead of *'more slowly'*.
But this is considered incorrect by some people.

1 How did they speak? Use the words in brackets to write true sentences, positive or negative.

1 Belinda (angry) _____ *did not speak as angrily as* _____ Charles.

2 Belinda and Charles (rude) _____ *spoke more rudely than* _____ Angela and David.

3 David (calm) _____ Charles.

4 Charles (polite) _____ David.

5 Charles (loud) _____ anybody.

6 David (nervous) _____ Angela.

7 Belinda (impatient) _____ Angela.

8 Nobody (impolite) _____ Charles.

2 Compare yourself with the people in the pictures.
First tick (✓) the true or false box for each sentence, then write some more true sentences.

	True	False
1 I never speak as angrily as Charles.		
2 I usually speak less impatiently than Belinda.		
3 I do not always speak as calmly as David.		
4 I sometimes speak more nervously than Angela.		
5 I do not often shout as loudly as Charles.		
6 It's good to speak as calmly as David.		

7 _____

8 _____

9 _____

10 _____

3 Write the word in brackets in the superlative form to complete the sentence.
Then use a tick (✓) to show whether you agree or disagree.

	Agree	Disagree
1 David spoke (polite) ___*most politely*___ of all.	✓	
2 Belinda spoke (angry) _____ .		
3 Belinda spoke (impatient) _____ .		
4 Angela spoke (nervous) _____ .		
5 People get angry (easy) _____ when they are tired or worried.		
6 In my family I am the one who gets angry (quick) _____ _____ .		
7 The people who win arguments are usually the ones who can speak (calm) _____ .		
8 The people who shout (loud) _____ are usually the stupidest people.		
9 The strongest people often behave (gentle) _____ _____ .		
10 People speak (polite) _____ when they are nervous.		

20 Irregular comparative and superlative adverbs

Irregular adverbs have the same comparative and superlative forms as adjectives.

Adjective	Adverb	Comparative	Superlative
fast	fast	faster	fastest
good	well	better	best
bad	badly	worse	worst

Other irregular adverbs are: hard – harder – hardest   soon – sooner – soonest
early – earliest – earliest   late – later – latest   far – further – furthest
little – less – least   near – nearer – nearest   much – more – most
long (time) – longer – longest

1 After the match. Some footballers are talking about a football match that has just finished. Rewrite the sentences so that they end with the words given.

1 I've never seen Peter play so hard before.

2 Nobody played as hard as John did.

3 Bob hasn't run as fast as that for a long time.

4 The match has never started as late as that before.

5 It's the first time we've had to wait so long.

6 Nobody played as badly as Ernie did today.

7 None of the other players can kick the ball as far as Tom can.

8 Dave doesn't usually argue with the referee as much as he did today.

9 Leon has never argued with the referee so little.

1 _Peter played harder than_ _____ ever before.
2 _John played hardest_ _____ of all.
3 _____ than usual.
4 _____ ever before.
5 _____ ever before.
6 _____ of all.
7 _____ of all.
8 _____ than usual.
9 _____ than usual.

21 Adverb or adjective comparison?

> He's a *safer* driver than I am. (safer = adjective)
> He drives *more safely* than I do. (more safely = adverb)
> Who makes *the fastest* cars? = Which cars are the fastest? (adjective)
> Who makes cars *the fastest*? = Who works the fastest? (adverb)

1 Adverb or adjective?

Write the correct words in each space to complete this quiz about languages.

1 Which are the two ____*most widely*____ -spoken languages in the world?

widest or most widely?

2 Which group of languages has the _____ verb forms?

most complicated or most complicatedly?

3 Is it true that most male Japanese speakers do not speak as _____ as most male Arabic speakers?

loud or loudly?

4 Is it true that people in Oxford speak English _____ than elsewhere?

more correct or more correctly?

5 Which is the _____ letter in the English alphabet?

most common or most commonly?

6 Which language has _____ sounds: English or Italian?

clearer or more clearly?

7 In which country are the _____ native languages spoken?

most or mostly?

8 The _____ living linguist, Georges Schmidt from France, can speak _____ than anyone else. How many languages can he speak?

greatest or most greatly?

languages more or more languages?

9 Do girls usually learn _____ than boys?

languages faster or faster languages?

2 Here are the answers to the questions in Exercise 1. One answer is wrong. Which one?

1 English and Chinese.   2 Some of the North American Indian languages.
3 Yes. 4 Yes. 5 e. 6 Italian. 7 India. 8 30. 9 Yes.

22 Quantifiers, adjectives and adverbs: positive and negative forms

Examples of positive forms	Examples of negative forms
Quantifier (much/many – more) I buy *more* books than you do (*more* used as a determiner). I've got *more* (than you) (*more* used as a pronoun). I like books *more* than you do (*more* used as an adverb).	You don't buy *as many* books *as* I do. You haven't got *as many* (*as* I have). You don't like books *as much as* I do.
Adjective (popular – more popular) Thrillers are *more popular* than classics. These are *more popular* books than those.	Classics aren't *as popular as* thrillers. Those aren't *such popular* books *as* these.
Adverb (quickly – more quickly) I read *more quickly* than you do.	You don't read *as quickly as* I do.

1 Nine of the sentences below come from a newspaper article about the kinds of books that men and women read. The information in one sentence is not true. Which sentence do you think is not true?

1 Romantic books are more popular with women than with men.
2 Romance is a more popular type of book than biography.
3 Thrillers are read more than classics.
4 Men read more thrillers than women do.
5 Men are more interested in humorous books than women are.
6 Men read more books about history (non-fiction) than women do.
7 Men enjoy violent stories more than women do.
8 Men read more classics and modern novels than women do.
9 Women read more biography than men do.
10 Horror is a more interesting subject for men than it is for women.

2 Write the nine true sentences in the correct negative form.

1 Romantic books are not as popular with men as with women.
2 Biography
3
4
5
6
7
8
9

3 Look at the diagram and answer the questions.
Write complete sentences comparing men with women.

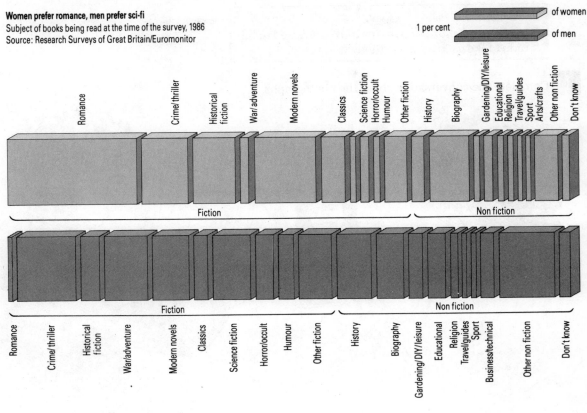

Women prefer romance, men prefer sci-fi
Subject of books being read at the time of the survey, 1986
Source: Research Surveys of Great Britain/Euromonitor

1 Do men read much science fiction?
   Yes. They read more science fiction than women do.

2 Do women read war stories much?

3 Do women read many historical novels?

4 Are men more interested in classics than women are?

5 Is adventure a popular subject for women?

6 Do women read much history (non-fiction)?

7 Do men read educational books much?

23 Verbal comparisons

> She's *older than* she looks.
> Cigarettes are *more expensive than* they used to be.
> It didn't take *as long as* we thought it would.

1 Complete the conversation about the photographs.

A That's Mary.

B How old is she?

A She's about 57, I think.

B Really?

A Yes. She's ¹_____ looks.

B What about John?

A He's ²_____ looks. He's only 23.

B John doesn't look very friendly.

A Oh, he's ³_____ looks.

B What's Mary like? She looks friendly.

A Well, she's the opposite of John: she looks ⁴_____

_____

What about *you* and *your* friends? Write two sentences.

1 _____

2 _____

2 The economic situation

Two politicians are speaking on television.
Write their sentences in a different way, beginning with the words given.

1 We are exporting much less than we are importing.

We are importing *much more than we are exporting.*

2 We used to work hard but now we don't.

We don't work as _____

3 We can't afford a high standard of living but we have one.

We have a higher _____

4 We should have planned our economy more carefully than we did.

We didn't plan _____

5 The government didn't intend to spend so much money last year.

Last year the government spent _____

6 The problem seems serious but it isn't really.

The problem isn't really _____

7 We thought prices would go up faster than they have.

Prices haven't gone _____

8 Things could be going worse than they are.

Things aren't going _____

9 The situation was bad but now it is better.

The situation isn't _____

10 Things don't look good now but they will soon look better.

Things will soon _____

24 Modifiers

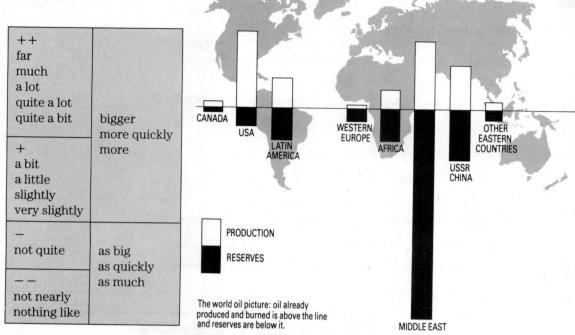

++ far much a lot quite a lot quite a bit	bigger more quickly more
+ a bit a little slightly very slightly	
– not quite	as big as quickly as much
– – not nearly nothing like	

PRODUCTION

RESERVES

The world oil picture: oil already produced and burned is above the line and reserves are below it.

1 Choose the best way to finish each sentence, according to the information in the world oil picture.

1 Canada's oil reserves are (a) slightly smaller than Latin America's.
    (b) a bit smaller than Latin America's.
    (c) far smaller than Latin America's.

2 The Middle East has not produced (a) anything like as much oil as the USA.
    (b) quite as much oil as the USA.
    (c) nearly as much oil as the USA.

3 Middle-Eastern reserves are (a) a little larger than any other area's reserves.
    (b) a bit larger than any other area's reserves.
    (c) far larger than any other area's reserves.

4 Compared with the USA, Canada has produced (a) nothing like as much oil.
    (b) quite a lot less oil.
    (c) a little less oil.

5 The USA has (a) slightly less oil than the USSR and China together.
    (b) not nearly as much oil as the USSR and China together.
    (c) not quite as much oil as the USSR and China together.

6 The USSR and China have (a) far more oil than other Eastern countries.
    (b) much less oil than other Eastern countries.
    (c) a bit more oil than other Eastern countries.

2 Answer the questions by giving the name of the country or area of the world.

1 Which country has quite a lot less oil than Latin America but a
   bit more than Western Europe?   _____

2 Which country has produced much more oil than it now has in
   reserve?   _____

3 Which area has not produced anything like as much as it has
   in reserve?   _____

4 Which area has produced a bit less than Latin America but a lot
   more than Canada?   _____

5 Which area has produced a bit less than the USSR and China?   _____

6 Which area has not produced quite as much oil as the USA?   _____

7 Which area has produced quite a lot less oil than the USA but
   quite a lot more than Africa?   _____

3 Fill each gap in this newspaper article with one word.
The information in the list will help you to choose the correct word.

Women are not represented well in parliaments around the world. This can be seen from the table on the right. Eastern European countries have 1 _____ more women MPs than the USA or Britain. The USSR and East Germany have 32% and Romania has 2 _____ more. Women in India are represented a 3 _____ better than in Britain, the USA and France but not 4 _____ as well as in Norway, Sweden and Denmark. Women MPs are 5 _____ a bit more common in most English-speaking parliaments than in Britain itself but 6 _____ like as numerous as in the Scandinavian and East European countries.

Percentage of women members of parliament in selected countries

Australia	10%
Britain	6%
Canada	10%
China	21%
Czechoslovakia	28%
Denmark	26%
France	4%
Germany (East)	32%
Germany (West)	10%
India	8%
Norway	23%
Poland	23%
Romania	34%
Sweden	29%
USA	6%
USSR	33%

25 Equal comparison

> **Examples**
>
> She is *as good* (a manager) *as* anyone in the company.
> She works *as fast as* the others.
> She works at *the same* speed *as* the others.
> She's *as tall as* she is clever.
> She is *the same* (height) *as* her brother.
> He eats *like* a pig.
> He tries *as hard as* he can.

1 Situations

Write what you would say in each situation, using '*as ... as ...*'.

1 A friend wants to stay in your house for the weekend.
Perhaps he would like to stay longer.

YOU: Stay **as long as you'd like to**.

2 At lunch time your friend does not take much food.
Perhaps he wants to take more.

YOU: Take _____

3 Your friend is planning to visit you again after two months.
Perhaps he can come sooner.

YOU: Come _____

4 You are taking your friend to the station in your car.
'Can't you go faster?' he asks.

YOU: I'm _____

2 *As* or *like?*

Use *as* or *like* to complete these common descriptions of people.

1 She's as light _____ a feather.

2 He smokes _____ a chimney.

3 That little boy is as good _____ gold.

4 He's always hungry: he eats _____ a horse.

5 She's as hard _____ nails.

6 I slept _____ a log last night.

7 He drives _____ a maniac.

8 He drinks _____ a fish.

9 After the party I was as sick _____ a dog.

3 | Jumbled sentences

Arrange the words to make sentences about people. Then write the sentences.

1 {is beautiful} {intelligent} {as} {she is} {as} {she}

_____

2 {stupid} {he is} {as} {is ugly} {he} {as}

_____

3 {she's} {person} {as} {as} {anyone I've met} {a} {nice}

_____

4 {a} {as} {father} {generous} {he's} {as} {anyone could wish for}

_____

5 {any that I know of} {honest} {he's} {as} {as} {a} {politician}

_____

6 {do} {smokes} {I} {heavily} {as} {he} {as}

_____

7 {strength} {he's got} {in his little finger} {as} {as} {much} {I've got in my right arm}

_____

8 {me} {as} {the} {almost} {height} {same} {he's}

_____

9 {he} {in the} {behaves} {his brother} {same} {way} {as}

_____

26 *Twice as... as...*

B is *three times as* tall *as* A.
B is *more than twice as* tall as C.

1 Reading

Try to *guess* which sentences are true and which are false. Or maybe you *know* the answers!
The sentences are all grammatically correct but only half of them are true.

	True	False

1 A mile is just over one and a half times as long as a kilometre.

2 A large python may be more than twice as long as an adult elephant.

3 A horse can go twice as fast as an elephant.

4 In Britain there are nearly three times as many cats as people.

5 In China there are nearly twice as many boys as girls.

6 The population of Africa is growing more than seven times as quickly as the
population of Europe.

7 In Japan there are nearly three times as many female bank managers as
male ones.

8 India produces more than three times as many new films as the USA.

9 The number of people in Europe under 16 is about twice as great as the number
of people over 65.

10 Travelling by car is twenty-five times as dangerous as travelling by plane.

2 The pay ladder in Britain

Use the information below to write comparisons about pay in Britain.

A High Court judge earns £70,000 per year
The Prime Minister   –   £65,000 per year
An airline captain   –   £45,000 per year
A surgeon   –   £33,000 per year
A university professor   £22,000 per year
A senior school teacher   £16,000 per year
A policeman/woman   –   £14,000 per year
(below sergeant)
A coal miner   –   £12,000 per year
A nurse   –   £ 8,000 per year
A secretary   –   £ 7,000 per year
A farm worker   –   £ 5,000 per year
A hairdresser   –   £ 4,000 per year

1 A surgeon / a nurse

   A surgeon earns more than four times as much as a nurse.

2 A policewoman / a secretary

   _____

3 A High Court judge / a surgeon

   _____

4 A university professor / a coal miner

   _____

5 The Prime Minister / a farm worker

   _____

6 A coal miner / a hairdresser

   _____

7 A coal miner / a nurse

   _____

8 A surgeon / a senior school teacher

   _____

9 An airline captain / a university professor

   _____

10 A policeman / a farm worker

   _____

27 Continuous change: *more and more…*

In Spring the sun shines *more and more* strongly
and the weather gets *warmer and warmer*.
More and more flowers appear.
Coats and umbrellas become *less and less* necessary.

1 Use these adjectives and adverbs to complete the sentences below.

interesting   fast   fat   painful   bad   fed up

1 I'm getting __fatter and fatter.__

2 I'm going _____

3 This book's getting _____ _____

4 I'm getting _____

5 The weather's getting _____ _____

6 My tooth's getting _____ _____

2 Changes in developed countries

Look at the lists of changes that are taking place in many countries; then write true sentences about modern life.

the price of computers

the number of people who attend church regularly

the number of people who work in factories

the smoking of cigarettes

the number of old people

the number of divorces

the number of cars on the roads

the number of holidays in foreign countries

1 Computers / becoming / expensive

Computers are becoming less and less expensive

2 People / living / long

3 Going to church / becoming / popular

4 Divorce / becoming / common

5 People / taking holidays abroad / often

6 Factories / employing / few / workers

7 Many / people / giving up smoking

8 The roads / becoming / crowded with cars

3 What other continuous changes are taking place?
Write about your country, about the weather or about yourself and your friends.

1

2

3

28 Parallel change: *The more … the more*

> **Examples**
>
> *The harder* I worked *the richer* I became.
> *The more* money I earned *the less* careful I became.
> *The more* I had *the more* quickly I spent it.

1 A romance

Underline the correct phrase in each of the brackets.

Alison first saw David at a party. She had gone to the party with
Ronald but he had met some old friends and was talking to them.
Alison saw David on the other side of the room. Suddenly he
turned and saw her watching him. She felt a little embarrassed
and looked away. When she looked again, he was walking towards
her. [1](The closer / Closer) he came [2](more she felt nervous / the
more nervous she felt).

   He introduced himself and they talked. They talked for a long
time, and [3](more / the more) they talked [4](she liked him more /
the more she liked him).

   They met again the following week, and again a few days later.
[5](The more they became friendly / The friendlier they became)
the more often she wanted to see him. [6](More often / The more
often) she saw him [7](the more happily / the happier) she was, and
[8](more she felt lonely / the lonelier she felt) without him.

   [9](Ronald the more he / The more Ronald) saw them together
the [10](more jealous / more jealously) he became. However,
[11](worse / the worse) he felt the less he said.

   Then Ronald fell in love with Mary, and everybody was happy.

2 Personal relationships

Complete the sentences and then say if you agree or disagree.

                                                                    Agree Disagree

1 If you get married early, it's better;
   in fact *the earlier you get married the better it is.*   ☐   ☐

2 If you are generous, you will be popular;
   in fact _____   ☐   ☐
   _____

3 If you have many boy/girlfriends, you will be happier;
   in fact _____   ☐   ☐

4 If you are honest, you will have fewer problems;
   in fact _____   ☐   ☐
   _____

5 If you smoke, you will be kissed less often;
   in fact _____   ☐   ☐
   _____

6 When you are kind, people respect you less;
   in fact _____   ☐   ☐
   _____

7 If you put a lot into a relationship, you get a lot out of it;
   in fact _____   ☐   ☐
   _____

8 If you are hard to catch, you will be more desirable;
   in fact _____   ☐   ☐
   _____

9 When you win an argument, you may lose a friend;
   in fact _____   ☐   ☐
   _____

10 When you love someone, you have fewer arguments;
    in fact _____   ☐   ☐
    _____

29 Popular sayings

1 For each of these common sayings a meaning is given below. Which meaning goes with which saying? Write the correct number in each box next to the saying.

A *Two heads are better than one.* 8

B *Blood is thicker than water.* ☐

C *Better safe than sorry.* ☐

D *Better late than never.* ☐

E *For better, for worse; for richer, for poorer;* ☐

F *The least said the better.* ☐

G *It's easier said than done.* ☐

H *Better the devil you know than the devil you don't.* ☐

I *The best things in life are free.* ☐

J *The grass is always greener on the other side.* ☐

1 It's better not to talk about it.
2 Take precautions.
3 An unpleasant but familiar situation is better than a new one.
4 It's a nice plan but not very practical.
5 Other situations always seem more attractive than your own situation.
6 Money does not buy happiness.
7 In every situation in life. (A man and a woman say these words when they get married.)
8 It's easier to find an answer if someone thinks with you.
9 Family ties are very strong.
10 Doing something late is not as bad as forgetting it completely.

2 Choose the best saying from Exercise 1 for each of these situations. Write it in the space provided.

1

2

3

4 A 'Everyone else is so much luckier than we are!'

 B '_____'

5 A 'I wish I were rich.'

 B '_____'

6 A 'My car doesn't go very well but I can't afford to buy a new
 one. Do you think I should sell my car and buy another old one?'

 B '_____'

7 A 'Tom's brother has never been nice to Tom; so why does
 Tom defend him when other people criticise him?'

 B '_____'

8

9

10

30 Idioms

1

Match the idioms on the left with their meanings on the right.
(Write a letter from (a) to (i) in each of the boxes.)

1 He's got bigger fish to fry.
2 Put your best foot forward.
3 All the best.
4 It went from bad to worse.
5 Better luck next time.
6 He's doing his best.
7 My better half.
8 I thought better of it.
9 He's bitten off more than he can chew.

(a) I wish you good fortune. (Usually when friends say goodbye)
(b) He's got more important things to do.
(c) He's trying to do too much.
(d) He's doing as well as he can.
(e) My wife. (informal and humorous)
(f) It became worse and worse.
(g) I changed my plan.
(h) Try to give a good impression.
(i) I wish you success if you try again.

1 ☐ 2 ☐ 3 ☐ 4 ☐ 5 ☐ 6 ☐ 7 ☐ 8 ☐ 9 ☐

2

Use the idioms below to complete the dialogue.

at least	as long as	not any longer	more often than not
more or less		the best of both worlds	at the most

A How much do you want for it?

B ^{1}_____ £2,000. It's in good condition.

A £2,000! It's worth £1,500 ^{2}_____ .

B Come on! It's a good car! Most cars are either bad and cheap or good and expensive; but this car's good and cheap. So you'll

get ^{3}_____ .

A Well, what's it like? I mean does the engine start easily on a cold day?

B Yes, ^{4}_____ .

A You mean it doesn't always?

B Well, it used to give a bit of trouble, but ^{5}_____

_____ .It's OK now ^{6} _____ you

remember to keep your foot on the pedal.

A I see. And it's ten years old, is it?

B ^{7}_____

3 In each of these situations write the most suitable idiom from the previous page.

1 Do you want to play football with us?

No. _____

2 I've failed my driving test.

_____

3 Richard's doing two jobs at the same time. He's getting rich but it's making him ill.

_____

4 I think the train is going to leave now. Goodbye John.

Goodbye Mary, and _____

5 I'm very nervous about my interview tomorrow.

Well, just _____

6 Who's that woman?

She's _____

7 Where's your new sports car? You told me you were going to buy one.

_____

8 Did you have good weather on your holiday?

No. It rained on the first day and then it _____

9 You don't seem to be making much progress.

I'm _____

10 Have you finished your homework?

_____ . I just want to check it.

11 Do you still live in London?

No, _____ . I've moved

to Manchester.

12 I've got a small flat in the city and a cottage in the country.

So you have _____

Answer key

Comparative adjectives

1 Short words and long words (page 4)

1 1 longer (or straighter) 2 straighter (or longer) 3 taller 4 more modern 5 faster 6 more expensive 7 more dangerous

2 2 are more ambitious than 3 are kinder than 4 are more interesting than 5 are more democratic than 6 are happier than 7 are more religious than 8 are more generous than

2 Spelling (page 6)

1
fit – fitter
thin – thinner
wet – wetter
sad – sadder

cloudy – cloudier
dry – drier
wealthy – wealthier
sunny – sunnier

bright – brighter
keen – keener
neat – neater
proud – prouder

safe – safer
free – freer
late – later
wide – wider

2 hotter, bigger, safer, uglier, flatter, faster, longer, wider, busier, deeper

3 3 but it's sunnier than yesterday.
4 it's finer than yesterday.
5 it's cloudier than yesterday.
6 but it isn't as cool as yesterday.
7 it's been wetter than yesterday.
8 yesterday was hotter.

3 Two-syllable adjectives (page 8)

1 1 (2) 2 (1) 3 (3) 4 (1) 5 (2) 6 (2) 7 (3) 8 (1) 9 (2) 10 (2) 11 (1) 12 (2) 13 (3) 14 (3) 15 (3)

2 1 (c) 2 (a) 3 (e) 4 (b) 5 (d)

3 2 more modern 8 more correct 9 easier 11 more careful 13 more exact 20 earlier

4 One- two- and three-syllable adjectives (page 10)

1 2 cheaper than that. 3 more useful than that. 4 smaller than that. 5 more special than that. 6 more necessary than that. 7 more informative than that. 8 more mechanical than that. (Lisa has bought a watch.)

2 3 that. 4 something funnier than that. 5 that. 6 something brighter than that. 7 something more delicate than that. 8 that. 9 something more modern than that. 10 something more useful than that. 11 something more romantic than that. 12 something darker than that.

5 *More* or *less?* (page 12)

1 1 Jenny 2 Peter 3 Sam 4 Hazel 5 John

2 2 Tennis courts are smaller than football pitches.
3 Walking is less tiring than running.
4 Playing tennis is less expensive than flying a plane.
5 Discos are noisier than cinemas.
6 Libraries are quieter than bookshops.
7 Wrestling is less violent than boxing.
8 Polo is less popular than football.
9 Motor-cycle racing is less peaceful than fishing.
10 Motor-cycle racing is more expensive than jogging.
11 A swimming pool is warmer than the sea.
12 The sea is less crowded than a swimming pool.

6 Negatives: *not as ... as* (page 14)

1 2 he isn't as attractive as Alfie Anderson.
3 he isn't as intelligent as Bernard Bjorg.
4 he isn't as young as Chris Carter.
5 he isn't as strong as Chris Carter.
6 it isn't as sensitive as Bernard Bjorg's.

3 2 (a) isn't as fast as the other one.
3 (a) isn't as convenient as the other one.
(b) is less convenient than the other one.
4 (a) isn't as long as the other one.
5 (a) isn't as famous as the other one
(b) is less famous than the other one.
6 (a) isn't as powerful as the other one.
(b) is less powerful than the other one.
7 (a) aren't as fresh as the other ones (as the others).

7 Irregular adjectives and quantifiers (page 16)

1 1 less 2 more 3 further 4 bad 5 fewer 6 worse 7 better

3 1 more 2 than 3 fewer 4 more than 5 as much 6 as 7 as/so many 8 as 9 more 10 than 11 as many 12 as 13 as little as 14 less than

8 Negative and positive comparisons (page 18)

1 1 better . . . than
2 worse for your health than sleeping too much.
3 Cycling is better for your heart than playing tennis.
4 Taking long holidays is healthier than working hard all the time.
5 eating a big meal in the evening is more fattening than having a big lunch.
(Peter is right every time.)

2 If you agreed with most of the sentences, you are probably ambitious and energetic. Success is important to you. But be careful: you are more likely to suffer from stress and heart problems than other people are unless you relax more.

If your answers were half and half, you are probably quite active and dynamic but still relaxed and not too anxious.

If you disagreed with most of the sentences, you are probably calmer and more relaxed than other people. However, if all your answers were 'disagree' you may be too relaxed!

3 2 Yes. Playing for fun isn't as satisfying as playing to win.
OR. No. Playing to win isn't as satisfying as playing for fun.
3 Yes. Being liked isn't as nice as being admired.
OR No. Being admired isn't as nice as being liked.
4 Yes. Cooperating isn't as enjoyable as competing.
OR No. Competing isn't as enjoyable as cooperating.
5 Yes. Driving safely isn't as important as arriving on time.
OR No. Arriving on time isn't as important as driving safely.
6 Yes. People who drive too fast aren't as bad as people who drive too slowly.
OR No. People who drive too slowly aren't as bad as people who drive too fast.
7 Yes. Chatting isn't as interesting as discussing work.
OR No. Discussing work isn't as interesting as chatting.

8 Yes. Lying on the beach isn't as good as visiting important monuments. OR No. Visiting important monuments isn't as good as lying on the beach.

9 Adjective or quantifier + noun (page 20)

1
2 with a lower collar?
3 with a smaller buckle?
4 with longer legs?
5 with a larger (bigger) handle?
6 with fewer buttons?
7 with thinner frames?
8 with narrower lapels?

2
2 such a high collar.   3 such a large buckle.   4 such short legs.   5 such a small handle.   6 so many buttons.   7 such thick frames.   8 such wide lapels.

3
The saloon car …
has got more doors than the sports car.
has got a bigger boot than the sports car.
hasn't got such comfortable seats as the sports car.
hasn't got such a powerful engine as the sports car.

10 Comparative adjective phrases (page 22)

1
2 as exciting to … with as
3 cheaper to … than
4 more expensive to … than
5 more difficult to … after
6 nicer to … than

2
2 safer to stand on and more convenient to store than other ladders.   3 cheaper to run and easier to park than other cars.   4 more comfortable to sit in and nicer to look at than other chairs.   5 more enjoyable to listen to and easier to carry than other personal stereos.   6 more exciting to visit and more difficult to leave than other holiday resorts.

Superlative adjectives

11 Adjectives of one, two and three syllables (page 24)

1
1 the heaviest   2 tallest
3 The most dangerous   4 the largest
5 most expensive   6 The oldest
7 The deepest   8 the longest
9 The most successful
10 The fastest   11 The loudest
12 The most intelligent

12 Spelling (page 26)

ACROSS: 2 closest   4 busiest   6 blue
7 hungriest   8 wise   9 thirstiest
13 softest   14 tamest   15 tight
16 slowest   22 lowest   23 wettest
DOWN: 1 biggest   3 sourest
5 stickiest   7 hottest   8 whitest
10 safest   11 simplest   12 fittest
17 wide   18 soft   19 few   20 hot
21 wet

13 Irregular adjectives and quantifiers (page 27)

1
1 the furthest   2 worst
3 the worst   4 the most
5 the least

2
1 the least   2 the most   3 best
4 the furthest   5 the most

14 Superlative adjectives: mixed types (page 28)

1
Room 1
warmest
noisiest
least sunlight
most comfortable
easiest to clean

Room 2
sunniest
most expensive
largest
most windows
nearest the kitchen

Room 3
quietest
cheapest
best view
smallest
best for working in

2
1 the cheapest   2 the best for working in   3 the quietest
4 the best view   5 the smallest
6 the largest   7 the nearest
8 sunniest   9 the most
10 the most expensive
11 the warmest   12 the easiest to clean   13 the most comfortable
14 noisiest   15 the least sunlight

15 Superlative or comparative? (page 30)

1
1 his brothers   2 as Charles   3 the family   4 the four   5 the brothers
6 as Edward   7 than all the others
8 of all

3
2 the furthest from   3 the hottest
4 closer to   5 not as hot as   6 the smallest of   7 the largest in   8 the closest   9 brighter than
10 the brightest

16 Superlatives and comparatives with *ever* and *never* (page 32)

1
2 the most uncomfortable chair I've ever sat on.
3 the worst hotel I've ever stayed in (at).
4 the laziest horse I've ever ridden.
5 the rudest man (person) I've ever met.

2
2 never sat on such an uncomfortable chair.
3 never stayed in (at) such a bad hotel.
4 never ridden such a lazy horse.
5 never met such a rude man (person).

3
2 (a) the most beautiful view I've ever seen.
  (b) never seen such a beautiful view.
3 (a) the most generous person I've ever met.
  (b) never met such a generous person.
4 (a) the most interesting person I've ever talked to.
  (b) never talked to such an interesting person.
5 (a) the nicest party I've ever been to.
  (b) never been to such a nice party.

17 *One of the -est* and *the second -est* (page 34)

1
2 people   3 is   4 second
5 person   6 some   7 words
8 the second   9 in   10 one
11 cities   12 is   13 largest   14 in
15 the largest

2
2 of the most common words in English.
3 He's one of the richest people in the USA (the world).
4 It's one of the most populated cities in the world.

3
2 it's the fourth longest river.
3 it's the third most populated city.
4 it's the second most common (the second commonest) word.

18 Zero article superlatives (page 36)

1
1 –   2 the   3 –   4 the   5 The
6 –   7 the   8 –   9 the

2

2 Venice is the most romantic city in Europe.
3 Paris is most beautiful in Spring.
4 September is the best time to visit India.
5 Australia is hottest when it is Winter in Europe.
6 Spain is the most popular destination for British tourists.
7 Americans, Germans and French people are the most frequent visitors to Britain.
8 Public transport in London is the most expensive in Europe.
9 The beaches of Europe are most crowded in August.
10 There is something interesting to see in most countries.

Adverbs: Comparative and superlative

19 Comparative and superlative adverbs (regular) (page 38)

1

3 spoke more calmly than
4 did not speak as politely as
5 spoke more loudly than
6 did not speak as nervously as
7 spoke more impatiently than
8 spoke as impolitely as (spoke more impolitely than)

3

2 most angrily   3 most impatiently
4 most nervously   5 most easily
6 most quickly   7 most calmly
8 most loudly   9 most gently
10 most politely
Note: It is possible but rather formal to use the article (the) with these superlatives.

20 Irregular comparative and superlative adverbs (page 40)

1

3 Bob ran faster   4 The match started later than   5 We had to wait longer than   6 Ernie played worst
7 Tom can kick the ball furthest
8 Dave argued with the referee more
9 Leon argued with the referee less

21 Adverb or adjective comparison? (page 41)

1

2 most complicated   3 loudly
4 more correctly   5 most common
6 clearer   7 most   8 greatest ...
more languages   9 languages faster

2

4 is wrong

Comparative structures with adjectives, adverbs and quantifiers

22 Quantifiers, adjectives and adverbs: positive and negative forms (page 42)

1

8 is not true

2

2 Biography is not such a popular type of book as romance.
3 Classics are not read as much as thrillers.
4 Women do not read as many thrillers as men do.
5 Women are not as interested in humorous books as men are.
6 Women do not read as many books about history as men do.
7 Women do not enjoy violent stories as much as men do.
8 Men do not read as much biography as women do.
9 Horror is not such an interesting subject for women as it is for men.

3

2 No. They do not read war stories as much as men do.
3 Yes. They read more historical novels than men do.
4 No. They are not as interested as (They are less interested than) women are.
5 No. It is not such a popular subject for them as it is for men.
6 No. They do not read as much history as men do.
7 Yes. They read educational books more than women do.

23 Verbal comparisons (page 44)

1

1 older than she   2 younger than he
3 friendlier than he   4 friendlier than she is

2

2 hard as we used to.   3 standard of living than we can afford.
4 our economy as carefully as we should have (should have done).
5 more money than it intended to 6 as serious as it seems.   7 up as fast as we thought they would.   8 as badly as they could be.   9 as bad as it was.
10 look better than they do now.

24 Modifiers (page 46)

1

1 (c)   2 (b)   3 (c)   4 (a)
5 (b)   6 (a)

2

1 The USA   2 The USA   3 The Middle East   4 Africa   5 Latin America   6 The Middle East   7 The USSR and China

3

1 far   2 slightly   3 bit | little
4 nearly   5 quite   6 nothing

25 Equal comparison (page 48)

1

2 as much as you want (to).
3 as soon as you can.
4 going as fast as I can.

2

1 as   2 like   3 as   4 like   5 as
6 like   7 like   8 like   9 as

3

1 She is as intelligent as she is beautiful.
2 He is as stupid as he is ugly.
3 She's as nice a person as anyone I've met.
4 He's as generous a father as anyone could wish for.
5 He's as honest a politician as any that I know of.
6 He smokes as heavily as I do.
7 He's got as much strength in his little finger as I've got in my right arm.
8 He's almost the same height as me.
9 He behaves in the same way as his brother.

26 *Twice as ... as; three times as ... as* (page 50)

1

1 T   2 T   3 F   4 F   5 F   6 T
7 F   8 T   9 F   10 T

2

2 A policewoman earns twice as much as a secretary.
3 A High Court judge earns more than twice as much as a surgeon.
4 A university professor earns nearly twice as much as a coal miner.
5 The Prime Minister earns thirteen times as much as a farm worker.
6 A coal miner earns three times as much as a hairdresser.
7 A coal miner earns one and a half times as much as a nurse.
8 A surgeon earns more than twice as much as a senior school teacher.
9 An airline captain earns more than twice as much as a university professor.
10 A policeman earns three and a half times as much as a farm worker.

27 Continuous change (page 52)

1
2 faster and faster 3 more and more interesting 4 more and more fed up 5 worse and worse 6 more and more painful

2
2 People are living longer and longer.
3 Going to church is becoming less and less popular.
4 Divorce is becoming more and more common.
5 People are taking holidays abroad more and more often.
6 Factories are employing fewer and fewer workers.
7 More and more people are giving up smoking.
8 The roads are becoming more and more crowded with cars.

28 Parallel change (page 54)

1
1 The closer 2 the more nervous she felt 3 the more 4 the more she liked him 5 The friendlier they became 6 The more often 7 the happier 8 the lonelier she felt 9 The more Ronald 10 more jealous 11 the worse

2
2 the more generous you are the more popular you will be.
3 the more boy/girlfriends you have the happier you will be.
4 the more honest you are the fewer problems you will have.
5 the more you smoke the less often you will be kissed.
6 the kinder you are the less people respect you.
7 the more you put into a relationship the more you get out of it.
8 the harder you are to catch the more desirable you will be.
9 the more arguments you win the more friends you may lose.
10 the more you love someone the fewer arguments you have.

Sayings and idioms

29 Popular sayings (page 56)

1
A 8 B 9 C 2 D 10 E 7 F 1 G 4 H 3 I 6 J 5

2
1 Better safe than sorry.
2 Better late than never.
3 For better, for worse; for richer, for poorer;
4 The grass is always greener on the other side.
5 The best things in life are free.
6 Better the devil you know than the devil you don't.
7 Blood is thicker than water.
8 Two heads are better than one.
9 It's easier said than done.
10 The least said the better.

30 Idioms (page 58)

1
1 b 2 h 3 a 4 f 5 i 6 d 7 e 8 g 9 c

2
1 at least 2 at the most 3 the best of both worlds 4 more often than not 5 not any longer 6 as long as 7 More or less

3
1 I've got bigger fish to fry.
2 Better luck next time.
3 He's bitten off more than he can chew.
4 all the best.
5 put your best foot forward.
6 my better half.
7 I thought better of it.
8 went from bad to worse.
9 doing my best.
10 More or less
11 not any longer
12 the best of both worlds.